ShArPI Model

The Art Of Listening!!!

A Guide To Advanced Communication

Foreword

What's the point?

The motivation to write this book comes from years of discussions with young people who were confused and frustrated about their inability to communicate with their parents, friends and family members. It also stems from parents who are adjusting to their children during their teen years. It was quickly discovered that adults most often do not know where to begin discussions in order to bond with young people.

The foremost complaint across the board is the powerlessness of getting the desired relationship; the second leading concern is ability to connect with others. Through my life lessons and training, I have gained unique insight that burns at the core of my persona and escapes during conversation or even during very simple daily interactions. The key element, often forgotten is self- assessment, constant self assessment on all levels.

Pretending to be engage in a conversation with one of my best friends for life (BFF), these pages were designed to invoke honest reflection. The reader will gain a truth that will forever change their life, because a change of mind will change a person's life. It is not a book filled with the usual "feel good" cliché moments, it is a time to be REAL. The reader with naturally contend with the decisions they have made so far and learn from them in order to improve upon them. In the end, a renewed freshness will be discovered.

Others perception and actions tend to become inhibitors to effective communication, ultimately leading to voids in relationships and poor self perception, these things have a direct connection to happiness. Why shouldn't the reader benefit from my life's experience? My story has shades of yellow and blue, when you mix them, they make green. This is the true reason behind the green logo of my non-profit organization, SharperMinds Consultants. A true blend of the good and bad, heartache and constant laughter, an assemblage of a domestic abuse survivor, failed relationships, a teenage mother who for several years raised a son who had been diagnosed with Mental Retardation alone and most notably an experienced police officer in a major metropolitan city. In fact, the popular television show The Wire clearly depicts what the early years of my law enforcement career and on the same streets. Through all of these experiences, the little girl who so desperately searched for acceptance emerged with an overwhelming feeling to share her "ah ha" moments.

What gives me the authority?

This book details how a little openness, mixed with a lot of creativity lends way to successfulness. Graduating from Baltimore City College High School, which is one of only a few prominent high schools within Baltimore City, earning two high school diplomas and the Mary R. Dudley Scholarships, obtaining an undergraduate degree in Psychology and Masters Degree in Education and being the second half of an amazing marriage, gives me the authority to write about the subject at hand. Not to mention, spending close to twenty years in the interrogation room, talking intensely with sex offenders and rape survivors have also afforded me the opportunity to develop keen listening skills and insightful communication techniques.

As a young person, my model of communication was distorted, learned by observing two people converse in the midst of two extremes, physical abuse or silently ignoring one another. In between the two extremes was a multitude of demeaning statements, harsh verbal exchange and constant blaming. However, I was fortunate to eventually learn that this was not normal or even acceptable. I decided to pray real hard and deal with family issues, what was revealed the biggest issue and the one at the forefront was the big communication one.

Open Communication

The first few years of my marriage was a transitioning time for both my husband and myself, we had to learn how to love and talk to one another and the rest just seem to fall in line. In fact, we publically acknowledge that we did not have our first real conversation until after we had been married for about one year in Deep Creek, Maryland. Can you believe that? The first conversation happened one year after we had been married, isn't that incredible? We decided to drive down alone, without family and/or friends and spend the weekend together. While driving through Maryland Mountains, we spent a lot of quiet time. We stayed at an old Monastery where Monks formerly lived and the sense of nostalgia forced us out of our personal corners and on to a platform facing each other, completely exposed. At that moment, we discovered one another's expectations and vulnerabilities.

Now, my husband and I host fruitful dialogues with one another. We respect each other's differences of opinions and have dedicated ourselves to truly demonstrating effective ways of communicating; the demonstration of mutual love is overwhelming. I am expecting that you will read this book and get a refreshing look at issues surrounding self appreciation and will also gain a better understanding of what it means to exchange ideas, listening to others, digesting what they are really saying and being an active part of the relationship. Most importantly, you will have learned what took me a lifetime; there is an art to being able to communicate with others; especially, when there seems to be so many extraneous variables to contend with, like emotions, preexisting issues and selfishness. Let us explore the Art of listening.

This book is dedicated to my handsome husband, Antoine "Honeybunny," and handsome sons, Andre, Love', Noah and Liam.

Table of Contents

Chapter 1: Say What You Mean & Mean What You Say!

In any relationship, parent/child, spouses, dating partners, schoolmates, co-workers and friends, there is a hierarchy of styles regarding verbal communication, ranging from most productive to least effective. They are **respectable conversation, silence, passive aggressive insults, debate and argument**. There are several forms of acceptable communication; for instance, we nod our head in acceptance. We wave our hand as a way of greeting one another. We shrug our shoulders to demonstrate that we do not understand, we offer compliments to strangers, we write inspirational thoughts; the list is perpetual.

Likewise, we converse with one another in varying ways, sometimes in loving traditions, sometimes in anger, sometimes while crying and sometimes in a whisper. When you are in a relationship (the type that have been outlined in the beginning), recognizing these various levels of communication is key to how effective you communicate with others. For the purpose of this book, relationships refer to the relationship between a child & adult, co-workers and dating relationships or even marriages. The subsequent chapters will detail more about how to have a discussion. At this point, it is more important to discuss ineffective communication styles, in order to identify problematic areas and deal with them.

Arguing is the most unproductive form of communication. For one main reason, physical altercation is usually the next threat following an argument. Even more so, it signifies a loss of control. In addition, in a squabble, name calling is tolerable, yelling is acceptable and no one is listening to anyone else. When people argue they are relinquishing hurt, pain and disappointment. Unfortunately, arguing usually perpetuates more of the same feelings and never leads to resolution. To paint a clearer picture, imagine a frying pan on top of an open flame. Now imagine adding teaspoons of water, a little at a time. If left on an open flame, the drops of water would bubble and eventually boil, then evaporate. However, if you remove the flame, the water will not boil but stay inside the pan until it eventually evaporates. The frying pan represents the non-aggressive person in the argument; the open flame represents the aggressive person, while the evaporating water is the hurt and pain caused by the argument. The drops of water represent verbal attacks and low jabs. The boiling water represents the vicious loss of control, moving about violently and out of control; whereas, if you removed the flame, the water would not boil out of control. Unfortunately, in an argument nothing is resolved, because it wasn't dealt with non-dramatically. The issues are not resolved! I had a co-worker who would constantly tell anyone who would listen about some of the mean things that she would say to her boyfriend. She would justify her statements, by saying that her boyfriend was not going to have the privilege of just speaking to her disrespectfully without her defending herself. When in fact, by arguing with him, she was allowing not only her boyfriend to speak poorly toward her, but she was minimizing her personal value by using such meager communication skills. She was inadvertently telling him that his reduced way of talking to her was acceptable and that she would give him a forum for it by engaging him in the same fashion. Like many people, she was sending a message by the way she communicated with him. Instead of arguing with him, she should have left the area, removed herself from his presence or stopped dealing with him all together. Instead, of arguing back and forth and then calling her friends trying to fortify herself, she should have used that energy to more properly deal with the issues in her relationship.

Recognizing that the other person is not your contender is the first step in successful communication. Many of us imagine a room filled with fans cheering on; this creates a fight response and makes us think that we are in a battle. We decide that we are "in it to win." Unfortunately, there is no winner in an argument and no crowd cheering us on. A loving relationship is never filled with quarrel and hostility. So, instead of tensing your shoulders and taking a defensive stance, stop those one-two punches. Just settle down and be the bigger person. Many self-help books discuss ways of being a better person; most of them suggest that refusing to engage in verbal battle is a great first step. People love to tell the story in which they are the hero, but how heroic is it to hurt a loved one? People argue as a way of getting attention, sometimes negative attention is better than none. They also argue as a form of distraction, to keep the focus away from something bigger. For example, a man might start an argument about his wife's poor house cleaning skills to distract her from his lack of attention toward her; while a woman might start an argument over a lack of intimacy, rather than discussing her own feelings of insecurity. A child might take out frustrations on a parent and co-workers often use each other as pretend punching bags to avoid dealing with home issues.

Another popular form of communication is the **great debate**. Many times, people spend time debating troublesome issues. However, debate is the second worse form of communication, because a debate puts a person in fight mode. The difference between an argument and a debate for the purposes of this book is that a debate is seemingly more civil, but with both, no one is actually listening. However, in an argument people are talking at the same time, while in a debate, one person speaks after the other, but the intentions mirror each other. Many times in a debate, instead of listening to the other person, while waiting to speak, people rehearse in their mind what harmful thing they will say next. Some people use the time when others are speaking as a time to reflect on some unresolved issue of the day, the week, a month, a year or even ten years ago. In fact, sometimes people start a debate just so they can relinquish some past hurt by their parents, co-worker, friend and stranger or even hurt that they had imposed upon themselves.

An example of a common debate is the one that discusses a person's unwillingness to answer the telephone. The debate begins with one person asking why the other didn't answer their call. The reality is, the moment in time had passed, the telephone was not answered and things moved on. It wasn't a life changing event. In fact, what the person was really trying to say to the other person is that they needed to hear that person's voice, feel comforted by them or maybe even share with them. Is it unfortunate that their mate missed the cue and was not available. The fact that they did not answer the telephone probably felt like rejection. Once these negative emotions have been triggered, an on slot of negativity is close behind and unresolved issues surface.

Debate should be avoided at all cost. Instead of engaging in a debate, try restating the points that are being made. Try saying say, "So you are saying, I make you feel like inferior when we debate in our arguments." By restating a person's words, you accomplish two things. You confirm that you heard what they were trying to say and it also gives you a chance to interject in the debate and calm things down, before it becomes a yelling match or an argument. Debates are consequential, someone always feels hurt or have regrets; constantly replaying the debate and thinking of things that they could have said to gain leverage.

Some people proclaim to despise arguing and debating. They will say that they avoid them, sometimes this is true. However, they insult others with the first opportunity. For instance, in some relationships, the wages of arguing or debating are too high. This occurs when the relationship is already unstable and any infraction may lead to both parties shutting down. Instead, a hurt person would wait until it is safe to criticize everything about the other person. When problems arise, they should be dealt with in this fashion. There should be a specific time designated to discuss the issues, the discussion should remain focused on the specific matter at hand and both parties have to agree with the discussion. If at any time the discussion is leading to an argument it should be stopped.

Chapter 2: When Girls Talk

As a tenured law enforcement officer in a major metropolitan area often leading in crime; having investigated hundreds of incidents where teenagers as young as twelve years old had been subjected to overt maltreatment, bullying, Rape, and physical violence to include being stab and strangled by their dating peers. Young people are dying at an alarming rate; they are in dire need of knowing how to set relationship boundaries and recognize the early signs of intimidation. On too many occasions, the opposing view of the interview table has forced a stare into the prepubescent eyes of some confused young girl who sneaked out the house to meet her boyfriend, only to find that she had to have sex with all of his friends, before she could leave or face the alternative and being beaten. Whether we are ready to accept this or not, teenagers are having sexual intercourse in the school hallways and the term "relationship" has been re-defined. For example, now if you have exchange more than two texts, you are in a dating relationship or at least that is the perception among teens. So, it is imperative they we protect them through education and awareness. Parents and friends have to learn to highlight communication cues in order to zone into the correlation to communication and a depleted self worth and even a tolerance for abuse. People do not feel connected, because they are not communicating.

My first hand knowledge comes from the host of young ladies that quietly tell me that they have been beat at my annual symposium on dating violence. It stems from the conversations that I have with my mentees that tell me that they know one or more classmate that is being beat at school. It is generated from my personal experiences as a teenage mother, who was beat, but had nowhere to turn; even more so, it comes from the innumerable adult survivors that started getting beat in high school and don't know how to break the cycle. I am pleading for a call to action at a very basic level, which is communication. To achieve this, it is important to understand what people are saying when they speak, especially girls, because statistic will overwhelmingly show that victims are females.

When girls talk they want to know that someone is listening. Females are natural sharers; they very willingly share many personal things about themselves. In fact, they are very open about what bothers them, makes them happy, their dreams and even desires. Cell phone manufacturers, I'm sure would agree that females spend more time talking and sharing with their friends, than they do spending time quietly alone self reflecting. Parents and dating partners are expected to understand females the most. Unfortunately, they are usually the ones who know the least about what moves makes. Girls spend all of their commuting time on the telephone with a girlfriend or close relative. While at work or school, she will probably share something personal with a co-worker. Females often tell the same story many times, for several reasons, to solicit approval from friends, gain support while dealing with difficult things or to share in hopes of discovering something new. When females share with their parents or significant others, she is attempting to bond and help them understand who she is. However, in many instances parents and dating partners listen up to a certain point. After a while, they become distracted and the words all sound the same. As sharers, by the time a female decides to share with their mate and/or parent, they have compiled many versions of their thoughts that have been diluted with input from every girlfriend, co-worker, parent and even stranger that has heard her problem and validated her point of view. So, what really happens is her point of view is never actually shared.

The consensus is that males and females are extremely different beings, but in actuality they are more alike when it comes to communication, with the exception of their style of delivery. Various types of verbal communication will be explored later. For now, it suffices to say, both females and males both want a receptive audience, the safety of expressing themselves without judgment and confirmation that they are making sense. In other words, females and males both want a listening engaged audience, who will hear what they are saying and share themselves. However, there are clear differences. For instance, males tend to be more assertive, direct and unyielding; while females tend to beat around the bush, make generalizations and excuse people for unwanted words or behaviors before addressing it. Have you ever noticed the amount of times, even in a heated argument when a female with take the passive stance; she offers justifications before expressing her point of view. For example, she may say "I know you have poor telephone reception in certain areas, but every time I call, you don't answer the phone." Her justification, which in this case is "poor telephone reception," excuses him from not answering her call and whether it's true or not gives him a way out. The "every time" part is a generalization and is wrong, because it sounds like he is under attack rather than addressing a specific action. In reality, she is really crying out to them to respond to her attempts to communicate with them. She would be better served to ask him if he wants her to call, if he is able to answer the telephone when she calls. She could also ask why doesn't initiate conversations by calling her. Females are really good at beating around the bush and indirectly addressing issues. The concern here is not him answering the telephone, but is a lack of communication between the two of them.

Even more so, when females talk to their mate and/or parents, she needs to be reassured that they are listening to her. There is an age old cliché, the story of a man watching television, ignoring his wife, while she is attempting to talk to him. It is almost humorous to watch. She grows more annoyed, while he continues ignoring her. When we give others the courtesy of listening, you give them cues that send the messages of approval or disapproval, tell them if they should continue talking and/ or if they should be silent. So people, listen to the young ladies when they talk. It will overall enhance your relationship.

So, should females stop talking with their mates and parents? No absolutely not, females just have to learn to start every conversation off, even the serious ones with something that will spike the other person's interest. If your dad or boyfriend likes sports, ask about the score of last night's game. If they like clothes talk about a nice suit that you think he would look nice in. If he likes politics, talk about it. Then ease into your main point, after you have met them on their level of interest. By doing this, you break through barriers that would normally put them on defense and enabled them to see you as a friend rather than a nagging mother. Yes, it would seem like you are perpetuating the trend of beating around the bush, but in actuality you are strategically setting the tone of the conversation.

Females have to fight the urge to start every conversation with their mate and/or parent by talking about themselves, their day, their girlfriends or even those new shoes. Make it all about them first, the rest is secondary. In fact, if a man's ego is stroked every time he talks to you, he will want to talk to you more. Likewise, if your parents find you have a common ground, they will want to talk and even listen to you more. You may find that they will not only start answering your telephone calls, but may initiate calls of their own. This seems like a tough thing to do and in fact, many will view this as too subservient, but it works. It may not be for everyone, but chances are the way you have been doing things did not work and there was a constant struggle to get attention.

Other things to avoid are excessive telephone calls, dealing with heavy topics every time you speak and sharing too much. For instance, if your cell phone bill is more than five percent of your bi-weekly income than chances are you are talking too much on the telephone. If your mate and/or parent knows all about your girlfriends problems and lives, than you are telling them too much. If your mate and/or parent knows every move you make throughout your day, you need more independence. The bottom line is to be an individual and not to get lost in the relationship web; privacy is a sure way to maintain healthy communication. This web happens when every aspect of your life is intermingled into your relationship. It's okay to keep some things separate. Talk more about what makes you happy and less about your girlfriend's new hair cut. They will appreciate you for not sharing every little detail about your friends, because they are not nearly as interested in them as you are. Similarly, your parent and/or mate are truly not interested in a heavy discussion every time they speak with you. Again, your mate and/or parent should be your confidant and sole supporter, but if every time they spoke with you they had to deal with some big deal breaking relationship matter, they would be petrified of speaking with you. It is important that they feel hopeful about the two of you rather than heavy.

Being right is often the driving force for females sharing and getting things out into the open. Females just have to say it and say it now; but actually it doesn't' matter who is right or wrong. What matters is that people hear you, when you speak. So keep it light, until that specially designated time comes when you are suppose to discuss the heavy stuff. Just like setting the tone, females have to create opportunities for real conversations with their mate and/or parents. Meanwhile, females should learn to work through things on their own and be their own listening board. The important point of interest here is the fact that others do not have all the answers and neither do your girlfriends. It is imperative for females to take the time to get to know their own self. By doing this, they can more effectively communicate with others; articulate their expectations share their hopes and get what they desire. Females should know that if they are not strong independent beings occupied by their own life, than they will quickly seem boring. Not to mention that all of their conversations will begin to sound the same.

At this point, it may seem like it is bad to talk to friends, co-workers and family members, about anything. However, it is okay to share, but focus on what brings happiness and growth. Females are naturally nurturing people pleasers. Why not direct time and energy discovering what makes your relationship thrive? Why not give others a chance to talk, this will eliminate assumptions. There is beauty in silence, which will be discussed later in succeeding chapters.

Chapter 3: What People Are Actually Saying

God gave us two ears, one to listen to words, the other to listen to the other person's heart. Actually, if females spent more time being silent, they could hear the other person's heartbeat. This is figurative of course, but seriously gaining a natural rhythm is important. It is also important to remember delivery & timing. It is imperative to understand that no matter how important the point seems, it is vital to plan the delivery of the information. For example, a payment for a school's field trip might be past due and if not paid, may prevent a person from going on the trip. Although, it is important to discuss this matter, it is inappropriate to have this conversation when your parent is capable of doing something about it. While they are at work, it is not a good time; they will most likely be focused on something else. It is also not a good time to discuss it in front of other family members or friends. You may be thinking, well when it is a good time? Surely it is not after the trip. It is better to discuss this matter during specially designated times. Chances are the other person is fully aware that funds are due and is planning to provide them. At breakfast, you might mention that the deadline is vastly approaching. The best way to handle tough conversations with others is to set aside a specific time to discuss them. Some household reserves Fridays as Pizza night and Sunday mornings for worship; likewise, there has to be a specific time to discuss the heavy stuff. The point is that difficult topics become more difficult, if they are interjected into already stressful times. I am not suggesting that complex topics be avoided; simply saying that what is the use in discussing something when it will not be well received or even heard.

Another important topic is delivery, delivery, delivery. The reason that people tune out, is because the delivery is all wrong. I recall being at a couple retreats, when the group was discussing relationships and communication. One woman in particular kept over talking this guy who was very anxious to get his point out. The two struggled for the audiences' attention for about ten minutes, when the guy had enough. He yelled in a hostile voice, "See, that right there. That stuffs a problem!" He was referring to her inability to keep quiet and allow him to speak. More importantly, he was referring to her delivery. In this instance, the group got quiet and everyone was put off by his loud outburst. However, laughter quickly filled the room, the males were laughing in support of what the man had just said; while the females were nervously laughing in an attempt to reset the atmosphere. Obviously the woman showed tremendous restraint, by not engaging him in front of everyone, but it was amazing how all of the other females so willingly received his disrespectfulness and allowed him to have the floor. Was it due to the subjective nature of females? Had they been taught to listen when a man yells? Or was it because it was easier at that point to listen to him, because he evidently had something important to say? As it relates to delivery, being loud and aggressive, as some people are when they speak is not only unproductive, but it is also counterproductive. People feel very territorial and will combat anything that they perceive as threatening. So the minute a person starts yelling, they have lost it. The conversation is at the point dead. Again, it is not necessary to retreat into a corner and let the other person yell, but here is where restating their points might come in handy. Another technique when dealing with a hostile or yelling person is to look them in the eye and quietly say, "You are upset. I will not allow us to fight like this. Maybe we should finish this conversation later." By doing this, you would have gained a chance to interject and re-direct the conversation. As well as, teaching them that you will not stand for disrespectfulness and/ or aggression.

The truth is people enjoy listening to their name being called and enjoyed hearing positive things about themselves. When this is not the case, their point is not received well. Therefore, find the good in people and compliment them. Remember names, try to avoid saying that you are not a "names person," wouldn't you feel a little put off if someone did not remember your name, but expected you to listen to them? It is essential to relay to others that we are actually listening when they speak. In other words, be quiet and listen even when you don't want to. Additional ways include nodding in agreement, holding a person's hand while they speak, remaining silent regardless how long it takes a person to get their point across, pretending that they are your best friend and imagining they are a lost child; these things will enable you to show interest and compassion for their ideas. It will show them that you truly care about their thoughts.

Now, considered the point of communication, it is usually to express a need. Often this need is to articulate an emotion or perception. Many times, people feel devalued by their peers, media messages and family members if they have to make the same point several times. This point can be observed in the hip hop culture of today, performer have gotten more dramatic with their appearance and music content. Everything seems to be geared toward the shock effect. Young girls are commonly called, "bitches", "ho" and "sluts". These derogatory terms have grown into a term of endearment among the younger group of adolescents that use them; in a sense they have come to represent acceptance, oneness and connection. This dangerous type of approval encourages females to go along with things like poor decision making and becoming involved in criminal activity, to fulfill those names. Desensitization to these terms is a direct reflection of unproductive peer relationships and negative self perceptions, both of which can precipitate victimization. The correlation between how a person allows others to address them and their self image is profound. Often times, adolescents feel compelled to live up to titles given to them by their peers or members within their family circles. More often than not, the unkind labels represent a lowered expectation; since it is easier to "go along with" others standard than it is to go against them.

Chapter 4: Choosing The Appropriate Type Of Phrase.

The bottom line is, stick and stones can break your bones, but words destroy your spirit. Once it has been said, it has been said! There are no do overs. It is so interesting that people who command attention when they speak are often the very ones that don't want to extend the same courtesy to others. I know, because for years I was guilty of this very thing. I am not sure why, but I felt like what I had to say was more important than others, or I already knew what they were going to say. However, after being wrong a lot, I realized that I do not have all the answers and now I actually learn from others when they speak.

There are many types of listening skills. Although many people have heard about active listening, not many people in reality do it. The first thing to recognize is that once you speak it; you have spoken it. You have extended a part of your mood, thoughts and emotions to the world. We learn very young that words hurt just as much as actions. Therefore, people have to think before they speak. In order to better understand this concept, it is important to understand varying types of phrases. There are at least four types of phrases in verbal communication, YAP or your approval (given), TAR arguing to argue, SAB sarcasms at its best and SAW seeking attention words. Although these types are not all inclusive, they nicely describe the most common conversations.

YAP (giving your approval)

EX. YAP: "I'll give you that. I did yell first."

The first YAP (giving your approval) can be used in two fashions, negatively and positively. In the negative sense, it is most commonly used when a person is attempting to maintain a level of superiority in a conversation. The example shown above clearly depicts that when this example is used, a standard has been set in the conversation. In fact, the other person is humbled and allowed to continue making his/ her point in a conversation only after getting approval from the aggressor. The problem is that the other person may not need or even want approval. It is not a good idea to assume that in order to move to the next level in a conversation, one person has to sign off on a certain point. Remember females want to know that their mate and/or parent is listening and want to listen, YAP phrases suggests that she is inferior and not on the same level; therefore, the wrong type of relationship is simulated. The other person may feel disrespected. Moreover, you just need to understand what the other person is saying and not necessarily "approve" what they are saying.

Let's be clear YAP phrases can be easily mistaken for restatement of the other's person's report for clarification. However, the two should not be considered the same. A restatement of an idea would be to simply say the person's statement in different words. Restatements are also followed by a question, asking confirmation that the statement has been interpreted correctly. For example, we can turn the above YAP statement into a restatement like, "You are saying I yelled first, right?" Rather than making a YAP statement, it is better to accept what they have said, apologize and move forward or agree to disagree and move forward. The key component is moving forward and getting out as much information or allowing the other person to get out as much as possible, so that latent issues are exposed. It is okay to move forward, without having resolved every single matter, because relationships are works in progress and many times, issues will constantly be re-visited before they are resolved.

<u>*Other examples of negative YAP statements.*</u>

For once, you are right. I yelled first.

Okay, I get it, you think I yelled first.

Yeah I hear you.

I'm just taking it all in.

I am listening, aren't I?

Good point, next.

YAP statements can also be positive, when used in a loving fashion. As with anything else, delivery is everything. Just like we discussed in chapter three, about what others are really saying, you must watch your style of delivery, to include body language, tone, speed, eye contact and type of phrase. These things are essential when using positive Yap statements, to ensure that they are not mis-interpreted. A positive Yap statement allows a person to know that you got the point, without them driving home the same point over and over. Many times, especially when people are aware that they have your attention, they do not like to surrender the floor. Even more so, people love to hear themselves talk and once they get started it is difficult to stop them. In these instances, YAP phrase are very effective with nudging that person on to the next point. An example of a positive YAP phrase would be, "Oh, okay I understand. I yelled first and that offend you." In most cases with positive YAP phrases, more words are utilized as a way of softening the message. It is important however not to become condescending.

Other examples of positive YAP statements.

You know, I yelled first and that was wrong.

What else did you want to add; I yelled and probably put you on defense.

I do hear what you are saying, maybe we can move to the next thing.

I'm just taking it all in, but I get what you meant.

I heard you clearly and you have a right to be upset.

That was a good point, what's next?

****

TAR (arguing to argue)

EX. TAR: "I yelled first. That's true; but you started talking to me first."

TAR (arguing to argue) statements are the most fun, because they can be found in any setting, private ones, and even professional ones. However, they are not fruitful when dealing with your mate and/or parent. When people use TAR statements they are attempting to be passive aggressive and could possibly be avoiding a more serious topic. Arguing to argue is a very unproductive form of self expression. For example, females tend to use this technique when there are underlying issues, but they are too serious to address, so everything becomes an argument. Mates and parents usually use these TAR statements to assure domination over the conversation.

TAR statements are popular with bullies and people who are afraid of allowing others to get too close to their true feelings. They use this statement to highlight others' shortcomings and keep the attention off of them. In effect, TAR phrases are distracters and absolutely unsuitable in a healthy conversation. TAR statements usually come in groups and will continue until the issues are resolved or the provoker is stopped. TAR statements are used to counter any and everything someone says just to get a reaction from them or deter them from continuing. Even with very simple TAR statements, they are usually projected in the form of questions and followed by some sort of justification. For an example, a mate and/or parent might say" How does that make sense? That is why I yell."

In order to avoid TAR phrases, accept responsibility for your own actions; don't think about extraneous variables, like some other pending matter. Additionally, don't respond to attacks and most importantly, remain focused on the matter at hand. It can become relatively easy to avoid TAR phrases, both using them and responding to them if this point is remembered, they don't have any value. Think of them as junk food, they just satisfy you for the moment, but in the end that give you excess weight and don't help at all. Why waste time arguing just for the sake of arguing, when time could be spent empowering your mate and/or parent and building a sound relationship.

Other TAR statements

Does that make sense to you? You wonder why I yell.

I yelled first, because you weren't listening, otherwise I wouldn't have yelled.

Why am I yelling? If I didn't you would not listen to me.

****

SAW (attention seeking words)

Whatever.

Is that right?

EX. SAW: "I tried to call you, but you must have been too busy with someone more important."

SAW (attention seeking words) are very popular among people who thrive off turmoil in their relationships. Since these phrases are never about the other person, but merely a way of keeping the focus on the attention seeker. There are a number of reasons why these phrases are used. For example, they are used to mask some dysfunction. In many cases, people are not able to talk openly about problematic issues; therefore, they use SAW phrases as a diversion. In addition, these phrases are also used, because they have been previously very effective with eliciting compliments or to reaffirm insecurities. Regrettably, this form of self loathing will deter positive mate and/or parents from sharing; for fear that the attention seeker will just bring them down or find away to redirect the attention back to them. Sometimes, SAW statements are used temporarily, but sometimes they are used long-term and become embedding in the core of a person's personality. They are however, unattractive and self serving.

People who need constant confirmation from their mate and/or parent and attempt to get it through SAW phrases are diluted about their mate and/or parent's roles. It is not the mate and/or parent's responsibility to make you happy or feel good about yourself. That is strictly a personal responsibility. SAW phrases tell the world that a person believes that they are not suitable for the world, they are in fact not good enough. They may believe this for a number of reasons, childhood adversity, they may have never really gained true acceptance from their parents or immediate social groups and/or they were done wrongly in their previous relationships. So, they feel like the world owes them something. Unfortunately, by using SAW statement, their mate and/or parents assume all of the responsibility for all the wrongs that they have experienced.

It would be easy to say that the attention seeking mate and/or parent suffers from low self-esteem, but the reality is all people often use SAW phrases at changeable times; primarily because all people crave approval and need attention. The problem with SAW phrases, aside from being very exasperating is that they give too much power to the other person. Meaning, another person should never be responsible for your self-appreciation. Conversely, when SAW phrases are used, they set a mundane tone in the conversation and in point of fact are deterrents to future conversations with the mate and/or parent rather than motivators. I recall having conversations with this teller at my bank, every time we talked, she was telling a story about how she wasn't pretty enough or skinny enough. Each time I shared a successful moment, she reflected on her life and what was missing. For example, I told her my husband and I planned on renewing our vows, but she wanted to talk about how she never had a formal wedding. I shared with her that I had just gotten a new professional stand-up kitchen mixer, but she complained about how she and her spouse could not afford one. I talked about throwing a baby shower for my sister, she complained about how her in-laws ruined her baby-shower. The point to this story is that it was my fault for continuing to share with a person who obviously would not be happy for anyone as long as she felt so bad about herself. So eventually, I stopped having conversations with her. I learned that she was not one of the most supportive people in my life and was dealing with her own issues. I learned to love her and understand who she was. The key here is I stopped sharing with her. Although, this change was acceptable for two associates who had seemingly grown apart, it would be detrimental in a couple/ parental relationships. The last thing you want is for your mate and/or parent is to stop sharing with you. When he or she stops sharing with you, they usually share with their friends or others. SAW statements don't hold a place in a healthy conversation. It is okay feel apprehensive or maybe even insecure, but that is an issue that you have to deal with, not your mate and/or parent. Since SAW phrases only force to people to give solicited not genuine compliments that they may not truly mean and/or makes them feel overexerted from

having to work so hard to build you up.

Other SAW statements

You okay? I am so tired of all this weight.

How is your day? My day sucks; I wonder why I have to work at this place.

You look so nice; I wish I could wear my clothes as nicely.

You always know what to say; I wish that I was smarter.

Chapter 5: The Beauty in Silence

The first thing I learned as a detective is that what a person says is not nearly as important as what other people think they said. Many people forget about the value of silence. It makes many people uncomfortable, but a lot can be learned during the quiet times. In fact, silent pauses are used as a way to elicit a response from the other person. For some reason, silence usually carries a negative connotation in relationships. The questions are always asked, are you angry? Why are you so quiet? You seem so distant, being so quiet. In fact, people are still communicating their emotions through their silence. Simply put, you can say a lot without saying anything at all. A lot of time is spent in interviews or interrogations, trying to figure out what a person means. Literal meanings don't hold a lot of weight in interviews. This means that carefully choosing your words and sometimes choosing not say anything at all is more influential, than saying the wrong thing. Technically, you can exhibit just as many emotions non-verbally as you can with words. The key here is to be silent for a good reason. For instance, you can be silent by ignoring someone, but this is not a good reason. You could be silent in response to question to show disrespect or disapproval, again that is wrong. You could be silent in an attempt to get attention from your mate and/or parent, but of course, that is also wrong. Some ways to be quiet for the right reasons are to be silent to actively listen, to focus on your emotions or to control your tongue and redirect inhibiting statements. Primarily, the best reason is to be silent in order to effectively communicate with your mate and/or parent.

One way to be silent, is to become an observer in every situation that involves communicating with others; especially the more stressful ones. It is easier to deal with things if you look at them from the other person's points of view. For instance, my sister and I would disagree often about cooking. Each day we would compete with one another, trying to make the best dinner. We would do this routine each day. In my opinion, I was the better cook, but in her opinion she was. We would get the family involved in our competition. One day we had a real conversation and it turned out that we were not only competing for the title of best cook; we were actually competing for several titles, best mother, best spouse, best friend and many others. Unfortunately, this conversation was not had until it was a little too late and our relationship suffered because of the inability to have real conversations. My sister and I have to work real hard daily to have a relationship. If we had healthy conversations like the ones that have been described, we could have avoided this hurt. If one of us would have been more silent, we could have identified the crux of the problem. We were fighting for each other's respect and acceptance. In fact, as the siblings with different mothers, we were really just trying to connect. Another example of golden silence can be found in a relationship I had with my ex-boyfriend. Each day, I would call when he got off work, but he would not answer. His would explain that the phone was in the car or he was unable to hear it because his music was too loud. I took it as a form of disrespect, thinking that he was purposely avoiding me. He knew I would be calling at this time and should have initiated the phone calls on his own. A lot of you may be shaking your head in agreement, but the reality is, I was actually checking on him. I would say, "You are a police officer and I just want to make sure you are safe." In a way this was true, because I was always expecting the hammer to fall or preparing for the worst case scenario. So, let me stop you from shaking your head in agreement, this routine was very unhealthy and always ended in an argument; in fact, the same argument for months. I dialed his number so many times that I got tired, by the time he finally answered, I was not only pissed off, but I no longer wanted to ask what he about his day; I just wanted an explanation for his non-conformity. He didn't call me, because he knew I would be calling. More importantly, I had conditioned him to perpetuate this unwanted behavior. You see, he knew what I was doing, because I broadcasted it. I was worried about where he was and what he was doing. He knew I would argue when he finally called and he was not going to call until he was ready. So, I learned to stop calling around this time, because I would not get an opportunity to speak to him anyway. Not to mention, if something horrible happened, I would know it soon enough and could not do anything about it. Instead, I used the energy that was once focused on him to meditate and pray. To thank God for the many blessings that he had given me. I learned to appreciate quiet time during the commute home and even thought about ways to improve my business. My fixation with talking to him was a form of controlling him. In the end, he called me everyday around his time to get off of work just to ask how my day was. When I stopped this negative communication, it improved the whole relationship. Nevertheless, the relationship ended and we are still friends.

Another example of a good time to be silent is right after you have had a disagreement with strangers, friends, relatives or co-workers. The first thing we want to do is call our "people" and tell them how we let the other person have a piece of our mind. We play up the story as if we had conquered the war. When we do this, we are seeking approval and confirmation for our actions. However, if our mate and/or parent failed to agree with us or give us kudos, we run the risk of transferring those same negative feelings to them. The best suggestion here is to be satisfied with our own heroic feelings and not seek endorsement from our mate and/or parents. Just assume they will be supportive and share the story with them after you replay the incident in your mind a few times and have taken a minute to use your own rationalization to dissect the matter. Listen more to your inner voice. In fact, sometimes our mate and/or parents use this time of excitability that people often have when they discuss incidents of their day to express hidden feelings that they may be having about you or to reiterate a point that they may have been trying to make. For instance, if you were accused by a co-worker of being too dismissive of others and you told your mate and/or parent; they might use this time to tell you that they agree with your co-worker. Without doubt, you will carry over the same argument that you had with your friend and/or co-worker. You might just let them have it.

Working in a male dominant profession has afforded me the opportunity to hear a lot of stereotypes about females; insecurities issues, lack of understanding and needing a lot of attention. I used to get offended hearing how derogatorily some of my colleagues would speak about their mates. After discussing this matter several times and defended the actions of females, some I had never even met, I learned to listen to my male counter parts and interpret what they were actually saying. What I learned was that most males do not hear anything their mates are saying past the first few words, when they are at work. They do not focus on their mates, but pour their energy into their job. They feel emasculated when their mates challenge them about their willingness to have conversations with them, send her flowers, working too much and so on. I learned that many males try to act more macho in front of co-workers and friends and present a very different self to the world than they do to their mates. They attempt to mask any personal feelings and will go to any length to keep their vulnerable selves private. So, it's no wonder the freely vent about their mates shortcomings, it takes the attention off of them.

My mentors have shown me that you have to decide what your goals are and work every day toward them. The art of listening ought to be a part of everyone's agenda. Your silent time can be used for reworking your emotions. Interestingly enough, silence is the key element in active listening. Followed by techniques to ensure that you heard what the person was trying to say, like restating their words and appropriately following-up to their questions or responses. My son is great with restating some things that I have said to him. At a very young age he began saying, "So, you mean..." This in turned forced me to speak slower and more clearly when I speak with him, which prevents me from having to repeat myself so often; as well as, being mindful that he is extremely literal. When he was about seven years old, I told him to take a shower. Of course he spent a lot of time in the bathroom, singing, playing and having a grand time. For him, it was playtime in the ocean. So after he got out, I asked if he washed up, with the biggest "ah ha moment" on his face, he said, "I'll be right back." He got back into the shower and spent even more time, when he got out this time; I asked again if he washed up. This time, he stuck out his chest and proudly said, "Yes I did." I asked, with soap and a wash cloth? He then had this peculiar look on his face and said, "I'll be right back." He returned to the shower, playing and singing. This time, he came to me and said, "Mom, I washed up with soap and a wash cloth and I am done, Look! You want to smell me?" So, I smelled his arm, it did not smell like soap. In fact, it was bone dry. I asked, "Baby, did you wash your whole body?" It was hilarious when he said, "I'll be right back." This became even funnier, when my youngest son was old enough to take his own showers and did the exact same thing. For a while, when I tell them it's shower time, I have to say, wash your whole body, with soap and a wash cloth, dry off with a towel and put on lotion. From time to time, I still hear, "I'll be right back."

Chapter 6: Timing Is Everything

Like with everything else, timing is essential with communication. Through extended conversations with people more experienced than myself in relationships, like elders and colleagues who have been married longer than me, I have learned that timing is everything. It is difficult to slow yourself down and set a pace. However, it is essential to dedicate to specific tone for conversations; this directly affects the quality of the conversation. Many things are included when setting the tone, like the choice of greeting, your mate and/or parent's availability and both parties' emotional state/ baggage is vital. Every conversation should start with a friendly or cute even flirty (for mates) greeting if possible. Humor will not only relax existing tension, but will also encourage others to be as sweet as you. In the beginning of our relationships, during the courting phase, my boyfriend (husband now) would always greet me by saying, "Hello, Mrs. America." My goodness, this is probably one of the reasons why I married him. He was so attentive and kind; not to mention, Mrs. America was a great compliment and regardless of how I was feeling prior to speaking to him, I always felt sexy after hearing that. As time progressed, Mrs. America changed to "My lovely Wife," and then to nothing at all during the rough times of our marriage; the times we like to refer to as our growing pains. However, I no longer wait to hear those things. Now, I initiate each conversation by saying "Hello, Caramel King", short for Big Daddy the Caramel King Mr., Sir. which is his pet name. In response, I usually get a warm receptive retort. Greetings tells your mate and/or parent whether to be on defense, prepare for a funny conversation or just to relax and let things happen naturally. Thus, before calling your mate and/or parent or answering their call, be ready to put forth your best self, just like in an interview or a meeting with your supervisor. You will ultimately train them to do the same thing. Many times, as is the case with my upbringing, models of effective communication is missing and people often learn as they grow. Unfortunately, this trial and error method leaves too much room to make mistakes and we have already learned that sometimes they can't be undone. Remember once it has been said, it has been said.

It is equally as important to deal with the accessibility to your mate and/or parent, or should I say understanding that you cannot control the accessibility that you have to your mate and/or parents. As I have shared, you could spend a number of years trying to get others to submit to your demands for availability. However, it is more productive to focus on the greeting you will give when you have their attention. Take time to discern through your own emotional state, it will work.

Setting the tone for a conversation is a little indistinct, so I will give you an example. I have been partner to a number of male police officers who have spent a lot of time explaining to their mates that they were held over at work, because they were speaking to a citizen or handling serious situations. It saddens me to see the frustration on their face and look of awe as they literally throw their hands up in the air. "She knows I'm a cop!" is usually the next thing out of their mouth when they regurgitate the story. Although, police officers availability is understandably compromised at times, due to the uniqueness of their profession, other professionals may not always be readily available as well. Clearly, the situation with the police officer and their mates is a non-resolute matter. It is what it is, so let us call their availability a mute point. Remember this the next time you attack your mate for not being available. Just rejoice in the fact that you have moments with them, take pleasure in that time. Make your time so enjoyable that others will want to be available for you, even when it is not convenient for them. Try not to spend one more minute discussing the other person's availability. You can't control what other people do and they will never measure up to your standards all the time; so, allow for exceptions. Don't transfer a feeling of a loss of control to them, get over it; it is not the end of the world.

Emotional state is the big deal in this chapter; we must get better control over our own thoughts and actions; stop blaming and looking to others for sympathy. Move forward and don't look back. SharperMinds motto, "Change your mind to change your life," was developed by happen stance. One day my best friends and I were brainstorming and having a discussion about the crux of my company SharperMinds. Initially, the company's slogan was "today's youth our responsibility", because the company's focus was to help youths through prevention and recovery of criminal involvement, victimization and poor decision making. Through our discussion we uncovered that the types of things that I was centering on like victim recovery and moving forward after adversity were all geared toward freeing yourself by training the way you think. In addition, we realized that this is something that all people could benefit from, not just youths. So we changed a few things. Now, changing negative thoughts to positive ones is the platform of my company and a common practice in my life. I intentional point out the brighter side to my family and friends when they complain to me about different things. I always try and find a positive notion. This helps me not to displace anger and temperaments. It has always been evident that dwelling on the past is unfruitful and time consuming. I hope that this book has given you a new perspective and be encouraged to try some of the techniques. Print the varying type of statement and be more aggressive with your listening.

This workbook encompasses experiences from a seasoned Special Investigations detective in a major metropolitan area, a perspective from a survivor of Dating & Domestic Violence and the inner voice of a thirteen-year-old in need of protection, love and acceptance.

ShArPI Model

Self Awareness
Hygiene
Self Esteem

Self Presentation
Anger Management
Conflict Resolution

Inter-Personal Relationships
Goal Setting
Interviewing Skills

One of the most effective ways to reinforce learning and highlight skills is to provide chances for students to marry what they have learned to real life application. The **ShArPI Model** counter attacks extraneous variables and embeds preventative measures that contribute to poor self images and negative decision making. This workbook provides several opportunities to develop skills by exploring real life scenarios that aid in the recognition of various healthy inter-personal relationships. In addition, learning is self directed and will lead to a renewed sense of self actualization; as well as, a working knowledge of community responsibility. Readers tap into their strengths and take ownership over their success. They compose vision boards, set goals and identify unhealthy relationship dynamics, by using this basic formula;

ShArPI Model=Recognize + Respond ◊ **Self-actualization**

A.   Recognize- healthy lifestyles, career possibilities, and socialization & inter-personal relationships by identifying inhibitors of positive self awareness.
B.   Respond- to negative influences past/present by setting goals to increase self preservation and development.
C.   Self-Actualization- Identify strengths and improve areas in need
D.   Move Forward- Dissect scenarios for real life application in order to become an important part of the larger community.

ShArPI Module-Hygiene

Step I

Purpose – This section will provide insight for the correlation between good hygiene and self-worth.

Activity- Use the space provided to outline your daily routine.

❖ In the morning, I get out of bed and _____

❖ I brush my teeth, (How many times a day?)

_____

❖ I will brush them in order to avoid,
(What are some things that may cause tooth decay?)
  o 1._____
  o 2._____
  o 3._____
  o 4._____

❖ I wash my body, (Please describe how often.)

_____
_____

❖ I wear cologne/ perfume, (What made your choose this perfume/ cologne)

_____
_____

❖ I select my own clothes, (What are some things that you think about while selecting your outfit?)

_____
_____

❖ I define hygiene as the,

_____

_____

❖ I define GOOD hygiene as,

_____

_____

_____

❖ Discussion -*Is there a correlation between hygiene and self-worth?*

_____

_____

The obvious answer is YES! People who are clean feel happier. People who take care with bathing and choosing outfits tend to connect more with others. Many times, people dress themselves as a way of expression. They take enjoyment when others compliment how nice they look and smell. Likewise, people who do not take care with hygiene and clothing spend time avoiding others. Often they feel unclean and this leads to them having a poor self perception. However, there are some things to consider, like affordability and family dynamics. So let us consider them.

❖ Does anyone in your family encourage you to wash every day?

❖ Does anyone in your family buy you perform/ cologne?

❖ Who purchases you clothing?

❖ Would you be willing to wash your clothes by hand to make sure they were clean, if an adult did not wash them?

Note- *"I knew a thirteen-year-old girl whose parents were getting a divorce. She had to be responsible very early and had to wash her clothing by hand. Sometimes, her clothing would not be as clean as her peers and this caused her to feel inadequate at times. She was picked on, bullied and teased. She did not have the resources to clean her clothing. The harmful teasing caused her to fail in school. She was a straight A student, but failed ninth grade History class, because she was tormented everyday in this class. She asked her teacher and other adults for protection, but no one responded. Eventually, she outgrew their name calling, but she needed to understand that she was special and had self worth. Self -worth should not be measured by clothing. It is just important to understand that you are special and by bathing everyday and taking extra care with your clothing, you will feel as special as you are."*

❖ **Write you're your thoughts about this.**

_____

_____

_____

_____

_____

_____

_____

❖ **What are some other things that would have helped her?**

_____

_____

_____

_____

_____

_____

_____

_____

❖ **What natural ways to scent you body and your clothing?**

_____

_____

_____

_____

_____

Take this time to research natural ways to make perform/cologne. Use this space to design your own fragrance, by using only natural products. *Ex. I love the smell of lemons, so I could make my own perform by squeezing a lemon into a spray bottle, adding water and spraying myself. What is your technique?*

_____

_____

_____

_____

_____

_____

_____

❖ **Self Assessment-** How did you feel completing this section? Did you get stumped at any time? Was it fun? Please make up a promise note to yourself about hygiene and say it every day. This note will become part of a larger Affirmation statement that will direct your thoughts.

****

****I PROMISE

TO _____

BECAUSE _____.

EVEN WHEN I DON'T FEEL LIKE IT,

I WILL _____.

TO SHOW MYSELF THAT I LOVE MYSELF. ****

Step 2

Purpose – This section will help build self esteem.

Activity- Use the space provided to define YOUR self esteem.

- ❖ The best (3) things about me are:

    - o 1._____

    - o 2._____

    - o 3._____

- ❖ I know this because people are always,_____ .

- ❖ I first noticed this when _____.

- ❖ Positive Talk- Let's be real honest, part of having a healthy self esteem is to identify areas that need improvement and work on them. It is not always ALL good.

- ❖ Name three things that you would change about yourself.

    - o 1._____

    - o 2._____

    - o 3._____

- ❖ Ex. I use profanity when I get angry.

    - o 1._____

o 2._____

o 3._____

❖ **Would you change these things, because you want to OR because someone told you they needed to be changed? (Please explain.)**

_____

_____

❖ **After identifying unwanted behavior, the way to change it is to replace it with better & more productive behavior. Using this formula, describe how you would change unwanted behavior, Recognize-Respond= Move Forward.**

❖ *Recognize*-Unwanted behavior-I use profanity when I get angry.

❖ *Respond-* I will take a moment and be alone the next time I get angry and then I will write down other ways of responding.

❖ Move Forward-We will discuss anger management shortly, but for now let us focus on self esteem. Use this chart to mark and follow the (3) things that you want to change.

Date	Response	When I first got angry, I felt…	Now that I have taken a moment, I feel…	I would like to try this technique again.

❖ Now design your own chart. First answer the next series of questions and then fill the information into your very own chart.

❖ **Recognize**-Write down something that you want to change about yourself.

_____

_____

❖ **Respond-** Think of some ways that you can change this thing.(Use this space below to outline them.)_____

_____

❖ **Move Forward-** Complete this chart.

Date	Response	When I ____, I felt...	Now that I_____, I feel...	I would like to try this technique again.

❖ **Remember-** If you cannot change it, you CAN change your perception of it? What will you change your perception of?

_____

_____

❖ **Discussion** -*Is there a correlation between self esteem and success in life?*

The obvious answer is NO! Just kidding the answer is YES!!! People who feel good about themselves draw people to them and exude positivity. Does this mean that you should skip around all day, happy for absolutely no reason? Of course not, it means that when we feel like we are our BEST selves, we give off an energy that makes other want to know what we know and be a part of our happiness. So let us consider them.

❖ **Do your friends and family encourage & compliment you?**

_____

❖ **Who is this person, please describe them?**

_____

❖ **Do you have a role model? If so, than who?** _____

❖ **Would you be willing to be your own role model?** Note- I met a young lady who was incarcerated and she wanted to own her own school. At each opportunity, she would role play and pretend to be the principal. Now, she has a life plan and clear goals that will aid her with starting her own school, when she is released from prison. This is awesome, because she will be released in three years and when we first met, she did not even know that there was greatness inside of her.

❖ Are you a role model? Do you realize that others are watching you? Everyday? Show people the good stuff that you are made of!!! Write down your definition of self esteem?

_____

_____

❖ Take this time to write your autobiography, feel free to add futuristic goals?

Who are you, what have you achieved or will achieve in life? What is your legacy? Will you marry? Will you divorce? Will you be a doctors, judge or teacher? Tell the world all about you.

_____

_____

_____

_____

_____

_____

_____

_____

_____

_____

❖ **Self Assessment-** How did you feel completing this section? Did you get stumped at any time? Was it fun? Please make up a promise note to yourself about having positive self esteem and say it every day. This note will become part of a larger Affirmation statement that will direct your days.

_____

_____

_____

_____

_____

_____

_____

****

****I PROMISE TO_____,

BECAUSE_____. EVEN WHEN I DON'T

FEEL LIKE IT, I WILL _____. TO SHOW

MYSELF THAT I LOVE MYSELF. I PROMISE

TO_____

BECAUSE_____. EVEN WHEN I DON'T

FEEL LIKE IT, I WILL _____. TO SHOW MYSELF

THAT I LOVE MYSELF. ****

ShArPI Module- Conflict Resolution/ Anger Management

Step III

Purpose – This section will reinforce anger management and conflict resolution techniques.

What is the vision for this section?

Young people are suffering and in some case are not gaining the proper knowledge to help them become productive citizens. They have been exposed to, are assailants and/or victims of some type of criminal activity. For this reason, the community has to try different approaches to reach them. This section will instil techniques to change poor behaviour and ultimate and/or parent ly help them become self actualized. Relying on several years of law enforcement and instructional methods; coupled with avoiding the usual cookie cutter approach provides a unique insight; with the belief that not enough consideration is given to non-traditional learners. In addition, consideration is given to varying extraneous variables that leads to and/ or inhibits understanding.

Activity- Use the space provided to measure your anger and response to conflict.

Have you ever wished you had done differently? How do you deal with things that make you upset? Before you get angry, do you feel other emotions? Is it too late to deal with Anger, after you become angry?

Conflict Resolution

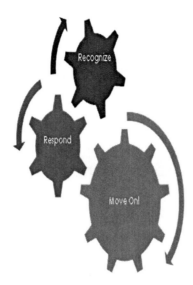

There are effective ways of resolving a conflict by employing SharperMinds Consultants 3 prong model.

"So a girl is tired of being on class, she decided to take a break. She walked to the vending machine and put in her last dollar, the machine accepted the money, but did not produce a snack. She pushed the button several additional times, still no snack. So then she grew very angry, kicked the machine, still no snack. Then she asked a classmate and/or parent for a dollar, she placed it in the machine and this time she got her snack. As she walked away from the machine, one of her classmate who was playing around knocked her into the wall and caused her to drop her snack. She felt anxious and angry. She needed to realize her anger, what should she do?

Recognize

The first step of resolving any conflict is projecting the likely ending. Although the person who generated the story about the girl and the soda machine is anonymous, it is a dynamic tool to illustrate the importance of respecting the likely ending. In this case, ignoring the likely ending yielded more frustration and wasted time.

STEP 1: Project the most likely ending.

SLOW DOWN. Really Slow Down and asses things; will you benefit in anyway by being involved in this conflict? What are some possible endings, consequences and/ or penalties?

Respond

STEP 2: Fight or Flight?

You decide. Look at things objectively. Be realistic and slow to react. After you calm yourself down, check yourself. Do you need a break? Retreating is okay, it may help you see things more clearly and not be bated into an anger episode. Address just the problem at hand, avoid saying "You always! You never! Not this time!" If you decide to engage, then do so wisely, rely on what you know and have practiced. Speak slowly and calmly. Use active listening and apply basic conversation skills, meaning allow someone else to speak and then you express yourself, not both at the same time. Be realistic, are you being effective if you are yelling, speaking offensively and antagonizing the other person?

Move On

STEP 3: Own your decision.

Time wasted is time spent on regrets. Be more proactive about your decision to be angry and learn from it. Again look at things realistically, you can be offended, but you are not allowed to live in that state. Dissect things, could they have been done differently. What things can you do to prepare for the next time? Should this thing be dealt with or should we move on from it. For example, if someone cuts you off in traffic, should you waste your time flipping them the bird or should you ignore the behavior. If you feel very strongly about it, report their aggressive driving to the police, if not let it go. Is it okay for people to mistreat you, no so choose not to be around them or find ways to effectively let them know you will not stand for their behavior.

Recognize: How to RESOLVE A CONFLICT

1. Take control. TAKE CONTROL OVER YOURSELF. Try to remove yourself from the situation. Express your feelings assertively.

2. Identify the reason for the conflict – Who is responsible? If it is needed, take time away from the person to think about the conflict and plan a strategy to resolve.

3. Communicate- Your emotions and feelings in a positive way. Trust me a person will listen to you, if you calmly express yourself.

4. Listen. Listen. Listen. Allow the person to respond.

5. Don't be afraid to leave until you calm down. It is okay to take a pause.

Remember: When I decide to have an angry outburst, I am telling the world, I am like a 4yr old unable to express my feelings in a healthy manner. I do not care who is effected, I need to be heard RIGHT NOW! I am the king of the mountain and would rather be by myself than with others. I will not slow down, I will not shut up....I have BOILED OVER!!!

****

****I PROMISE TO_____,

BECAUSE_____. EVEN WHEN I DON'T FEEL LIKE IT,

I WILL _____. TO SHOW MYSELF THAT I LOVE MYSELF. I

PROMISE TO_____

BECAUSE_____. EVEN WHEN I DON'T FEEL LIKE IT,

I WILL _____. TO SHOW MYSELF THAT I LOVE MYSELF, I

WILL _____. I HAVE SELF CONTROL. WHEN I FEEL LIKE I

AM OUT OF CONTROL, I WILL _____. I PLAN TO

PRACTICE _____TO MAKE SURE THAT I STAY IN

CONTROL OF MYSELF.****

STEP IV

Goal Setting- Identifying Obstacles, Overcoming Barriers &

Have you ever set a goal? Did you reach it? What is standing between you and your goal? How can you achieve your goals? Is it too late to achieve your goals? Why is it important to have goals? What can you do well? What gives you pride? Courage and motivation? Short term VS long term goals, different? How will you reward yourself for achieving your goals?

Recite Affirmation Statement/ Pledge

Recite the Positive-Talk Mental list (the ones they produce in Self-Esteem Section…. I love my teeth, I love hair, I love that I'm silly, etc.)

Create a list of possible careers.

_____

_____

_____

_____

Now write down things that could/have stop you from reaching those goals. (Boredom, Distraction, Finances, Lost Hope)

_____

_____

_____

_____

_____

Identify short and long term goals, completing the attached goal worksheet.

- ❖ What do you like to do?

- ❖ Identify obstacles;
    - o *Ex. I want to be a singer, but it does not pay well and I have a family to support.*

- ❖ Overcome obstacles;
    - o Ex. I cannot be full time singer, but I will join the church choir.

- ❖ Accepting your obstacles;
    - o Once you have identified obstacles, determine if you can change or get around them.

Ex. I cannot be full time singer, because I can't sing. The singing lessons have not helped. Although, I really love singing, I will have to be a songwriter instead.

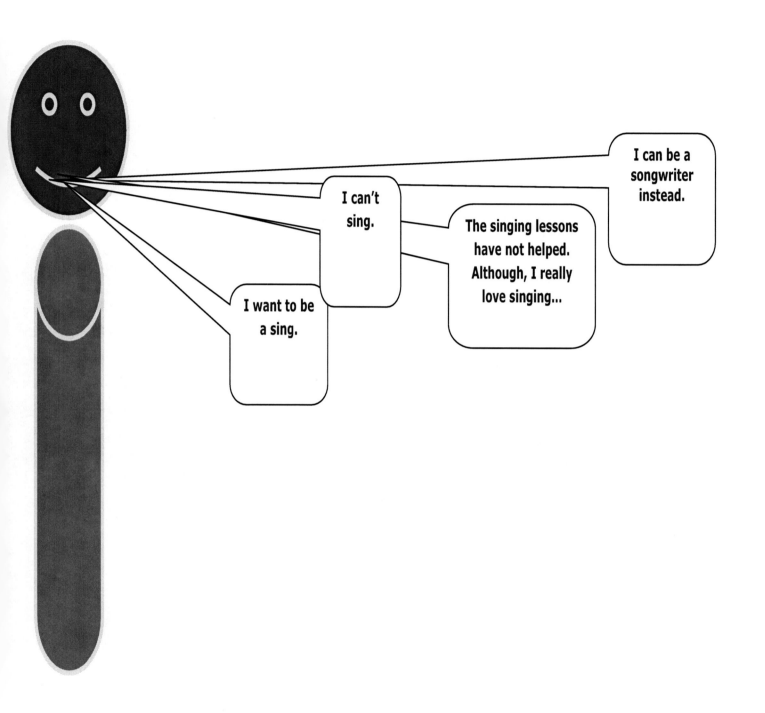

Worksheet

Identify Obstacles

Lets Talk about it!

1.	Why are goals important?
2.	Why are obstacles important?
3.	
4.	**You can reach your goals, if you constantly remind yourself of them!!!**
5.	*Ex. I will finish reading a self- help book.*

Identify 3 short term goals.

1. That deals with behavior.

   a. I will not swear for (3) months

   _____

   _____

   _____

2. That deals with change of mind

   a. I will not have negative self talk.

   _____

What does Self-Esteem have to do with Goals?

You can reach your goals, if you constantly remind yourself of them!!!

Ex. I will finish reading a self- help book.

Identify 3 short term goals.

1.   That deals with behavior.

   a.   I will not swear for (3) months

   _____

   _____

   _____

2.   That deals with change of mind

   a.   I will not have negative self talk.

   _____

3.   That deals with academic or skill set.

   a.   I will read a book.

Goal	Obstacle	
Start my own business.	Not able to work, because of age.	

Student Worksheet 2

Write down short term goals & the obstacles beside it. Then share them with an adult.

Goal		Solution
Ex. Start my own business.	Not able to work, because of age.	a. Write a book about starting your own business.
1.		
2.		
3.		

The purpose of a short term goal is to take small strides toward a long term goal. They are important, because they keep you motivated, because you feel successful when you accomplish them. They also help maintain focus.

As we transition toward long term goals, let us focus on these aspects.

1. **Dream or Reality:** is it realistic to think that you can achieve your goal.
2. **Seriously:** Do you need to rethink things? Should you add to your goal, re-define it?
3. **Go For It!** What is it, your game plan? What are your short term goals that are going to help you? How will you stay on track? Are you keeping track of them?
4. **Get it Done!!!** Get rid of those obstacles!!!

Goals	Dream/ Reality	Seriously	Go For It	Get it DONE!!!
I will graduate from school and become a doctor.	I can get a high school diploma and continue on to college. Eventually, I will obtain a PHD/ Doctorate.	I need to determine what type of doctor I would like to be. I prefer working with children, rather than working with senior citizens. I can be a Pediatrician.	First, I need to go to class. Then I need to get good grades. Then I must learn the requirements to be a doctor.	

Goals	Dream/ Reality	Seriously	Go For It	Get it DONE!!!
I will graduate from school and become a doctor.	I can get a high school diploma and continue on to college. Eventually, I will obtain a PHD/ Doctorate.	I need to determine what type of doctor I would like to be. I prefer working with children, rather than working with senior citizens. I can be a Pediatrician.	First, I need to go to class. Then I need to get good grades. Then I must learn the requirements to be a doctor.	

Develop your Life's timeline

6mos.   12 mos.   3 years   5years   10 years

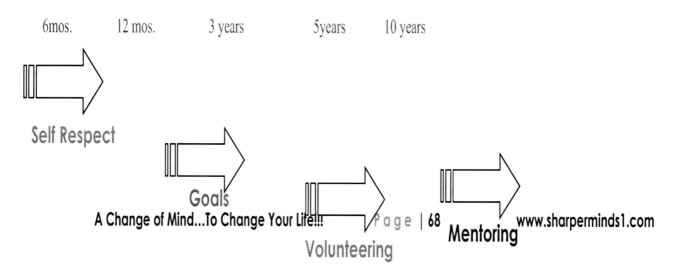

Self Respect

Goals

Volunteering

Mentoring

Lawyer

The ShArPi program relies on an analysis called an Instructional Systems Design (ISD). Traditionally, an ISD has been described as a "set of procedures that, when applied to an instructional goal, results in the identification of the relevant steps for performing a goal and the subordinate skills required for a student to achieve the goal." (Instructional Design, 2010) In other words, the instructional analysis highlights how well participants interpret the intended messages. Each Phase of the SharPI Program has a different objective, which directly correlates to the overall goal of facilitating problem solving, critical thinking, improving self-esteem, bettering self awareness and improving communication with adults. Research shows that teens lose interest in school for many reasons; they are struggling socially, they are losing interest in other things as well, they are struggling academically, learning disability, they may be being bullied, substance Abuse (drugs or alcohol), family situation has distracted them from caring about school, a boyfriend or girlfriend might be distracting them, peer pressure and an overall lack of interest. (Battle & Love)

****I PROMISE TO_____,

BECAUSE_____. EVEN WHEN I DON'T FEEL LIKE IT, I WILL

_____. TO SHOW MYSELF THAT I LOVE MYSELF. I PROMISE

TO_____ BECAUSE_____. EVEN

WHEN I DON'T FEEL LIKE IT, I WILL _____. TO SHOW MYSELF THAT I

LOVE MYSELF, I WILL _____. I HAVE SELF CONTROL. WHEN I FEEL

LIKE I AM OUT OF CONTROL, I WILL _____. I PLAN TO

PRACTICE _____TO MAKE SURE THAT I STAY IN CONTROL OF

MYSELF. I HAVE A VISION FOR MY LIFE; MY BIGGEST GOAL IS TO

_____. TO ACHIEVE THIS, I WILL _____,

_____ AND _____.****

ShArPI Module- Interviewing Techniques

Did you know that your classroom is preparing you for your future? Everything that you learn today will be used again, even Math

skills. There are several teachable moments in life. Let us embrace this one!!! You have to get into the business of selling yourself, even if you plan to work for yourself.

❖ Please describe what you think an interview is-

_____

_____

☐☐☐☐☐☐☐☐☐☐☐☐☐☐☐☐☐☐☐☐☐*My definition- An interview is a time for you to present yourself in your best light and*

to show how you match the job, school, etc.

Pre-Interview

What are things to consider?

1. **What to wear**?

    a. Wear a black suit, black shoes and neatly groomed hair.

    b. Now is not the time to be fashionable, be conservative.

    c. Shoes should be comfortable and flat.

        (I love high hills more than anyone else that I know, believe me I would wear them to bed if I could. However,

        they do not have place in the interview room.)

    d. Perfume should be light and refreshing.

2. **Body Language**

a. The hand shake- Extend your right arm, thrust your right hand forward, and grab the interviewer's left hand. Place the web of your hand into the web of their hand and grasp firmly. Shake once and then let go.

b. Eye contact-While shaking the interviewer's hand, look at them in their eyes. Do not stare, but do not look away first. It sends a message that you are capable and confident when the other person looks away first.

c. Posture- Stand straight, pretend you are in etiquette class with a stack of books on top of your head. While sitting, keep a straight posture; place your hands in your lap and/or on the chairs edge. Avoid touching your face and fidgeting.

d. Stance- Stand in a comfortable position, with your feet shoulder length apart and a slight bend to your leg. This will allow you to stand for a long period of time, without appearing that you are uncomfortable and will minimize your desire to fidget and move unnecessarily.

e. Elbows-Did you know that if you kept your both of your elbows bent during the first half of the interview, you probably did not have a great first half of the interview. Think about it, if your elbows are bent, that means that your hands are raised to some level and are probably distracted your interviewer. Try this, bend your right elbow and occasionally bend your left one. You might, interlock your fingers or lay one hand on top of the other.

3. **Speech**- Speak properly. If you usually use slang and broken English, practice speaking properly before the meeting. Be natural, do not use words that you do not normally use in an attempt to sound intelligent, it may have the reverse effect. Also, speak slowly. By nature fast paced speakers tend to sound rushed and preoccupied.

4. **Cell Phone-** Does not have a place in the interview room. Leave it in the car or turn it completely off. While waiting to go into the interview room, please silence the ringer. A ring tone can tell a lot of unwanted information, which can send the wrong message to the interviewer.

5. **The Room-** If the room has more than one chair for interviewees; ask the interviewer where you should sit. Do not make assumptions. If there is only one chair, take a seat after the interviewer takes a set, and again do not make assumptions. You want to display your manners at all times. Look around the room for personality indicators. For example, if you see a Ravens football mug, you may want to tell the interviewer that they are your favorite team. However, keep your comments generic; do not make comments about family pictures.

6. **The Entrance/ Exit-** Walk in with a sense of accomplishment, as if you already were accepted and/or were offered the job. Thank the interviewer for seeing you and open with a joke to break the levity. There are many jokes on line, use one of them to help make you memorable. Before you walk into any interview room, prepare by learning the about the institution and/or company. GOOD LUCK!!!

7. **Be prepared-** Know what your goals are. Write them down. Don't be afraid to talk about where you want to be in the future. Tell the interviewer why you want the position or to attend this school. Talk about briefly about competitor companies and explain why you did not select them. After all, it is your choice to show up at this company for the interview.

··

Mock Interview-

❖ Interviewer- "So, I am looking at you and at least one hundred other people just like you to be the project manager for a video shoot of local singer. Why should I select you?"

 o Start by re-stating the point of the interview.

 _____

 _____

 o Match your skills with the interview. *(It is okay to **accentuate** them.)*

 *ex. I am very organized, so I know I can handle this. I helped organize my family reunion.*___

 _____

 _____

 o Be ready to talk about area that you need to improve. It is okay to be honest, but not okay to bring your weaknesses up first. Respond to this question and then make up your own.

 "I noticed that you did not have a lot of experience, will this be a problem?"

 _____

 _____

 ⬜⬜⬜⬜⬜⬜⬜⬜⬜⬜⬜⬜⬜⬜⬜⬜**Now make your own**

 List your question here.

1. _____

2.

3.

Respond here

1.

2.

3.

Name five times when you would be able to use interviewing skills.

1.   4.

2.   5.

3.

ShArPI Module- Effective Inter-Personal Communication

Part III. Dating Relationship Interviews

Based on what you have learned about school/ job interviewing techniques, design a set of questions that you would ask

someone with whom you are in a relationship with. Here are a few suggestions.

1. ☐☐☐☐☐☐☐☐☐☐☐☐☐ When you get angry, how do handle it?

2. What would your friends tell me about you?

3. How would you describe your communication style?

4. What qualities do you look for when you select your friends?

5. Do you always have the same type of friends?

6. Do you always have the same type of disagreements?

Refer to the *ShArPI Model, The Art of Listening- Effective Communication* and describe your communication style. Provide examples.

❖ I prefer _____ statements, because _____.

❖ I tend to use _____ statements when I am _____.

❖ _____ statements are best used when _____.

❖ My hero _____ uses _____statements.

❖ Although I have a tendency to use _____statements, I will try to utilize

_____ more often.

Rates these words in order of importance in a conversation.

First	Right	Agree	Disagree	Purpose	Respect	Listen	Finish
12345678	12345678	12345678	12345678	12345678	12345678	12345678	12345678

Please rate them first, before proceeding to the next page.

This is the order they should be in.

Purpose	**Respect**	Listen	Agree	Right	Disagree	First	Finish

Defer to the book, *ShArPI Model, The Art of Listening- Effective Communication* for details about the subsequent key points.

The purpose of any conversation should be understood by both parties. To define the purpose, tell the other person what you think the purpose is and see if they match.

Practice

❖ For the next 24 hours, start every conversation off like this sample and see how things change. *"I would like to have a conversation with you about* _____."*

❖ Now write down any differences that you observed with how you felt during the conversations and what cues the other person gave you about the conversation.

     o Were you more relaxed?

     o Did the other person seem more willing to listen?

     o Did you have to re-visit the purpose of the conversation?

     o Did the purpose change?

     o How many conversations did you have with the same purpose?

Respect

❖ When dealing with inter-personal communication, many variables have an impact. Even before the first word is said, one must consider the non-verbal cues and body language. Mutual respect is key.

o   Write down five ways that a person can show respect.

- ▪
- ▪
- ▪
- ▪
- ▪

❖ **Please list them first, before proceeding to the next page.**

This is what I learned in life; there are five simple, yet important ways to show respect;

1. Eye Contact

2. Facial Expression

3. Hand movement

4. Being attentive to the other person

5. Using respectful language

The bottom line, if you would prefer not to have others disrespect you, you must respect others.

Acknowledgments

My life has been filled with many ups and downs, dynamic moments and fantastic people who have shown their support in many ways. Every day is a bundle of laughs. In fact, before they had reality shows, I would say to myself, "I could not have written a better script." I would follow that up by saying, "I need my own reality show." In this new millennium, as I sit on my deck, with my husband's head laid on my thigh, I feel the breeze of the peaceful wind and marvel at my journey up to this point. I see Andre "Dre," lounging on the chair beside us, spinning his key chain and asking the same question (over and over again), it is humorous. He is such a sweetheart, having been diagnosed with Mental Retardation; he can't help but to keep asking the same questions. So we keep answering, the same question (over and over again). He is such a bright young man and loves his brothers so much. I also hear Liam's voice trickle in from the basement. He is the smallest one with the strongest will. He calls out to Noah, "PLEASE Help." Inevitably moments later he always says, "I am not a baby!" It reminds me of all the times I relied on my older sister Kandy and little brother Larry for help, when we were growing up. Even though it got really rough at times in our household, we always loved and protected each other. Thank you guys, we made it out!!! No more yelling. No more fighting and finally no more public humiliation. Noah, just like Kandy, leaps at the opportunity to help and protect his brothers. I remember one time in particular, I was in elementary school and was being picked on by this bully. I made it a point not to tell my sister, because I knew she would beat her down! I was a bit shy and just did not want to make any trouble. For such a pretty girl, my sister Kandy was always very tough and could throw a punch like a man. Must be that Martins blood running through her veins. If you are from Baltimore, especially the south side, you probably know and love a Martin. So, anyway, back to this bully. She was in a grade or two higher than me, she kept picking with me. I let it slip to my sister. Kandy ran around to the side door, where that bully was coming out. Kandy grabbed her in the collar and said, "You better leave my sister alone!" The bully look so intimidated, she not only left me alone, but even apologized. She never said two words to me or my sister again. I loved having an older sister. In fact, I love all of my siblings, including Niecy, Timika and Morgan. I also love my sister-in-law Katina who helped mode me into a better listener and a more understanding woman by allowing me to vent, talking me through difficult times and never judging. Thank you girls, thank you Larry; life would be less fun without you. Now, I should not breeze pass my brother Larry, "Lil Larry," the cutest thing in the whole wide world. He has always been the nicest person that you ever wanted to know, always making jokes. My fondest memory of him was around the times of my parents' divorce when we were all going through so much turmoil. Instead of focusing on his own pain, he ministered in the street to neighborhood guys who just wanted to hang around. I have always adored his faith and love of Christ.

Writing this book was necessary; it allowed me to reflect on all the people that GOD put in my life. I will speak a lot about GOD, because for me he is everything, even before I realized how much he was blessing me, he was blessing me. There were many angels in my life's path that helped direct my steps. One person in particular stepped in and assumed the big brother role when I so desperately needed it. He bought my first back pack, when no one else seems to even care if I went to school. This person encouraged me to continue to go to school, sometimes filled with hunger and shame from growing up in dysfunction. He was a great facilitator for forgiveness. In fact, he was one of the first people to make me reflect about why things happen the way they did. Thank you Adrienne "Audie" Murphy, you will never know how much you impacted my life. Mornique, Mia, Tasha, Tanya and Aunt Kandy, Tikie and Tori, you guys were also right there, pushing me along and serving as symbols of a loving family. Uncle Mark, what can I say you are embedded in my memory as a great God Father and awesome big brother. You represent everything good about men. Also Jeryl, I would be remised if I did not mention you. You cared for Dre when he was first born; you cared for both of us. You guys are awesome leaders.

I have also been blessed to have had so many loving friends that knew me at varying points in my life. Although there are just too many to name, I have to acknowledge my Baltimore City Police Department family. Shantel, remember the times? One time we were on foot patrol on Monument Street, we were in the process of making an arrest of two men for a narcotics violation. After we got the handcuffs on one, one of the guys ran off. Without hesitation Shantel took off after him and I grabbed hold of the other one. It is important to note that Eastern District was notoriously known as the most dangerous part of the city, at that time and people did not hesitate to fight police. Almost as a reflex, police officers protect each other's lives, like it was our own. I had my guy in handcuffs and Shantel was off running down the alley. Worried that the runner may have been armed and/or wanted on a warrant, I immediately began to run my suspect down Monument Street to my patrol car to secure him and catch up with Shantel. I threw him the back seat of the patrol car and jumped in to find Shantel. When I got to her, she was dragging the runner out the alley, with the meanest mommy look I had ever seen on her face. It was one of the funniest moments in my police career, because I was so relieved to see that she was okay, but by the look on her face and his, I knew I should have been far more concerned for his safety than hers. Oh man, my adrenalin is flowing right now remembering all the funny times from the Eastern District. To reflect on all of them requires way too much time, so I will save them for another book. The word "Secure" took on a whole new meaning to my partners, Booker, Brian and Ruff Ruff, you guys are hilarious. Timberlake, Tilson, Fries, Chez and Weems, remember Latrobe Projects, all the action; sector One was the best. Even my times in Special Investigations built lifelong relationships, Stoner & Matt, thanks for putting up with my mess, they were my work husbands. You have to be a cop to fully understand what that means; it is when you build a bond with your partner, that you can finish each other sentences in an interview. Griffin & Stinnet, you guys are my little brothers, Justin I will pray for your patience to deal with Griffin. Merryman, John, Rob, Mike, Derrick and Boobie, I will never forget our time, it was so much fun. The all night stake outs and long hours to get the guy, we worked like a fine oiled machine. Dee White, Kiesha, Barbara, Risa, what can I say? We need "Sha-Bang time,"

I have to acknowledge my BFFs who always keep me grounded, Michelle, Angel, Shelly, Stephanie, Lorraine, Sunny, Shantel, Tracey, Rhonda and Sage (not in any order); you guys are beautiful and filled with kindness and laughter. Thank you for helping me laugh at myself and giggling with me. To talk about our moments requires a whole other book, too many moments, to many good times. Most people get one chance at having a good friend, but I must admit I have had plenty. You all have left an impact on my life that motivates me to be more honest and self revealing.

My professional motivation has come from many mentors, who I consider friends, but there have been a few special ones who gave me a chance, when I didn't even believe in myself. They allowed me to grow into a good detective and a life-long learner. Namely, Sergeant Booth, Major Magness, Major Barillaro, Sergeant Jones, Sergeant Morgan, Attorney (Retired Major) Hill and Division Chief Stanton. I am incredibly grateful to you all. You all taught me all you knew and allowed me to flourish on my own. Let me just say, Mrs. Stanton is a beast in the court room and Barillarro I remember when you stayed up with us until 3:00 am. You were on the other side of the interrogation room, sliding questions under the door, when most supervisors would have been home sleep; thank you ladies for showing that maternal love; as well as, being strong leaders. Before I close this part, let me tell you about the Parent Teacher Fellowship Board, I am the president, but Shelly, Jocelyn, Tony and Aleshia you guys kept me in stitches, we work so hard every day and every day I laughed out loud about something that you guys said. One phrase comes to mind, "Party People!!!" You all are more like family.

My cousin April Yvonne Garrett, what can I say? You took our family to Kenyon, Columbia and Harvard. You "Amplified Baltimore" to new heights; most of all you broaden my perspective and showed me that I could be powerful. You are my hero! Cuzo

Stephanie, you have always been right there, such a strong person. To be one of the youngest in the family, you are definitely one that brings so much love and cohesion. Thank you girlie, you represent us well.

A special acknowledgement goes to my parents, Larry Martin Sr., Angelo & Ann Chatmon. Even through our difficult years, you managed to support all of my efforts and always remained behind the scene. Mommy, we have a special unbreakable bond and somehow I wanted to be successful for both of us. Your selfless acts of kindness, prove that you are one phenomenal lady that I only aspire to be like. Thank you for allowing me to be first. Mommy, I remember the time you furnished our home. We had all these beautiful pictures on the wall and mirrors, all the latest leather furniture. I also remember how those things were destroyed from you and dad breaking what he didn't sell. I feel so sad remembering the looks on your face as you tried to hold it all together. I know how hard it must have been for you to raise us and go through the things you did. I LOVE you for all you did and continue to do. I also know your heart and your story, please know you are great! You are amazing and you are the best mom we could have wished for. Thank you. Dad, I love you to. You had an addiction and some issues. I pray for you and wish that you could have lived a much happier life. Despite your issues, you were so funny and charismatic. Angelo you were there for Mommy and us, you are so cool. Thank you for loving my Mom and making her happy.

Lastly, my best friend and charming husband, you showed me true love, through your abilities to connect with all types of people. You are just a nice guy. I have become better at seeing the good instead of the bad in all situations. You came into my life twelve years ago, became daddy to my special needs son, and gave me three more amazing son. The years of happiness between us mean everything to me. I never understood what gave you the ability to always see the glass half full, but now I understand. Thank you, "Big Daddy, The Caramel King, Mr. Sir" for teaching me to be a good mother, woman and wife. You are my very BEST friend in the whole wide world. I can be overheard echoing, "I got a husband, I don't have to …" It's because of the safety and security that makes me say those things. THANK YOU! Man I love you.

Most importantly, GOD thank you, you have shown me favor and blessings. I love you and hope that you will use this book to give others acumen and peace when they learn to love themselves and communicate this love to the world.

Thank you. Please visit **www.sharperminds1.com** for additional readings.

CPSIA information can be obtained at www.ICGtesting.com
Printed in the USA
BVOW020926261011

274465BV00003BA/1/P